Perfect SURF

IMAGES OF WESTCOUNTRY SURFING

JON BOWEN

HALSGROVE

First published in Great Britain in 2008

British Library Cataloguing-in-Publication Data
A CIP record for this title is available from the British Library

ISBN 978 1 84114 827 4

HALSGROVE
Halsgrove House
Ryelands Industrial Estate
Bagley Road, Wellington,
Somerset TA21 9PZ
Tel: 01823 653777
Fax: 01823 216796
email: sales@halsgrove.com
website: www.halsgrove.com

Printed and bound by Grafiche Flaminia, Italy

Introduction

When someone mentions UK surfing, they usually mean Westcountry surfing. Devon and Cornwall are not the only places to get waves in England, but they are the most well known and it is here that surfers are the most spoiled. Sticking out into the Atlantic ocean we are unprotected from the undiminsihed open ocean waves powering into the weathered coves and open beaches. These primeval swells wrap themselves into the convoluted folds of the coast, themselves formed by the same wave energy over millions of years of erosion and attrition in a near eternal cycle of modification. Travel in any direction except one in Devon or Cornwall and you will hit the sea, with exposed coast in all directions meaning that whatever the conditions of wind or tide there will almost certainly be somewhere with a surfable wave. Away from the surf meccas of Newquay or Croyde are a multitude of secret spots, some difficult to find or access, others just requiring enough sense of adventure to leave the well trodden paths to the more famous surf beaches. It's this that I've tried to capture in this book – no famous surfers, no well-known spots, just a cross section of the grassroots of surfing, and ordinary surfers trying to fit in the eternally addictive thrill that is wave riding around life's obligations of work, food and sleep, whenever and wherever they can.

Acknowledgements

Thanks as ever to the surfers of Devon and Cornwall
for being such willing subjects, and to Rosanna Rothery
for being inspiring, encouraging, beautiful and wonderful.

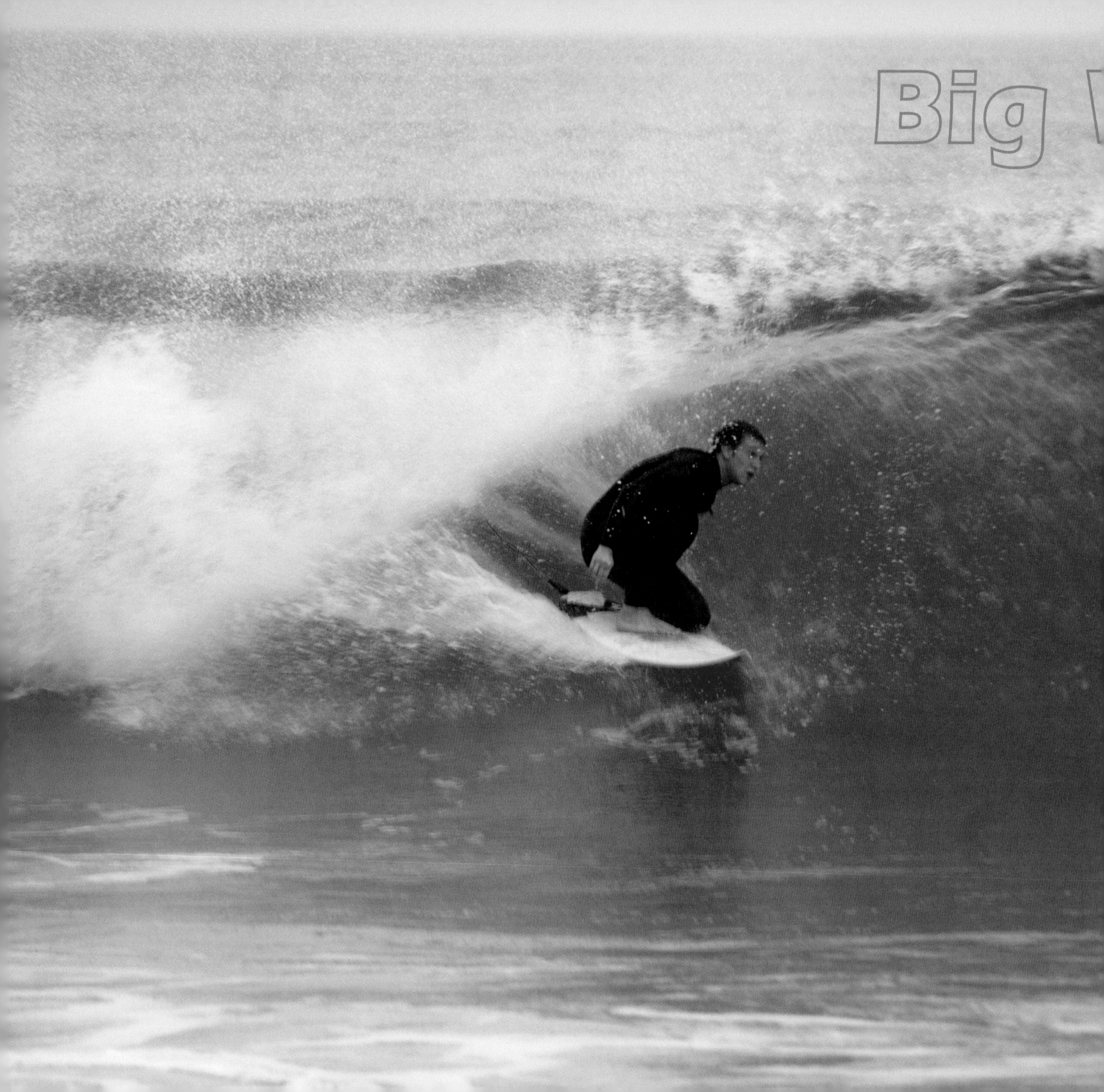

Big

aves Big Waves
Big Waves
Big Waves

Big waves propel surfing into another dimension. Riding giant waves changes the sport from one of fun and exhilaration into one of fear and trepidation. During the winter when deep low pressure systems come barreling in from the Atlantic, the offshore reefs with cryptic names – Cribba, Oysters, Daggers – start to work. Big wave riding requires its own equipment, long narrow sleek boards known as guns, built purely to control the speed generated by hurtling down the face of a double-overhead wave. These boards are devoted entirely to getting into the wave, getting down the face before the lip falling behind you overtakes you and drives you under. It also requires a different mindset from the surfer. He must control fear and ride to survive, racing the tons of water falling behind and over him to the safety of the channel. The enjoyment comes later from the joy of being alive and then the chance to do it again!

mility Humility
Humility
Humility
Humility

Humility

Surfing is a sport that does not match athlete against athlete, but the individual against the infinitely larger power of the ocean. Because it is an obscenely one-sided contest you can only approach surfing with a degree of humility and acceptance. You must accept that you are the weakest element in this battle and that the sea is merciless and impersonal. If you paddle out in conditions which you can't deal with then you will not receive any favours from the sea. You may love the ocean but it cares nothing for you and its power and strength are relentless and unforgiving. To give yourself over to something that dwarfs you, and to tap into its extraordinary limitless energy just to ride waves is one of the joys of surfing.

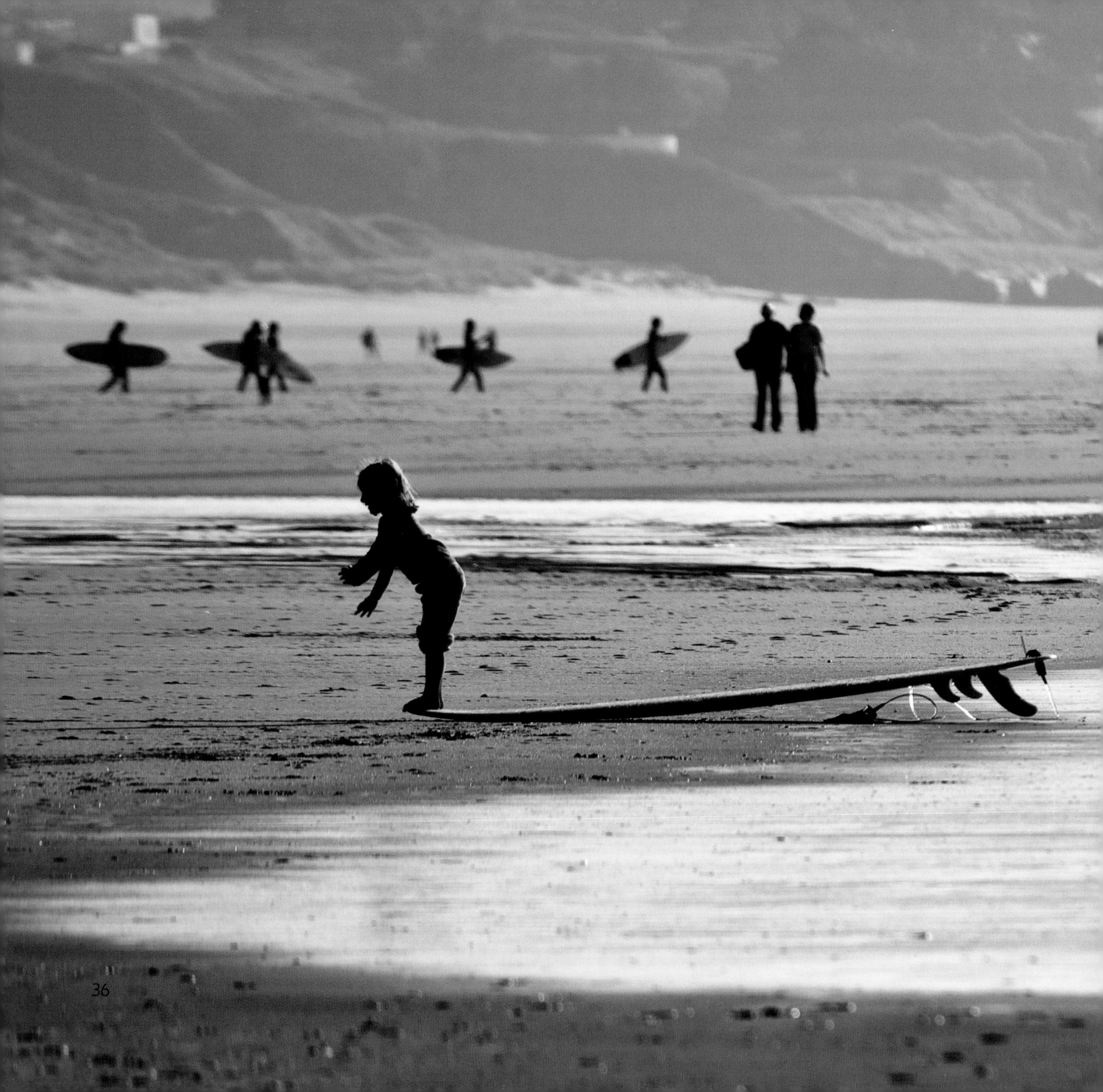

Every Wave's a Party

y than Rich Lucky than Rich

Lucky than Rich

Lucky than Rich

Surfing is largely about luck. To ride a wave you need a combination of skill and strength, but to find the waves in the first place, you really need to be lucky. In the last decade or so surfing has become awash with money. It's no longer surprising when you see expensively dressed men turning up at the beach in gleaming BMWs with boards on the roof, but you can't buy yourself waves. You can increase your chances, certainly. You can jet off to obscure Tahitian islands, or you can bask in the luxury of an air-con boat while you cruise through the Indian Ocean, but that's no guarantee. You can spend thousands and travel further and find nothing. Or worse, while you're away you could miss the day of the year back at home that the minimum-wage slaves you left behind scored. For the surfer, it's better to be lucky than rich.

49

61

Micro Waves

Waves Micro Waves Micro Waves

Big waves are fun to ride, but small waves are fun to look at. It's difficult to judge the size of a wave without something, or someone, to scale it against. Every surfer has paddled out at an empty break and found themselves surprised that it was bigger, or more usually smaller, than they thought. Watching waves that are centimetres high peeling perfectly along a miniature point or sandbank, it's difficult not to imagine yourself minituarised and being able to ride them, mind-surfing your way into tiny barrels or dropping in on micro-wedges. On a flat day watching these tiny images of scaled-down perfection while you wait for the next low pressure to send in their bigger brothers is a summer torture.

CuttieCuttie
Cuttie Cuttie

74

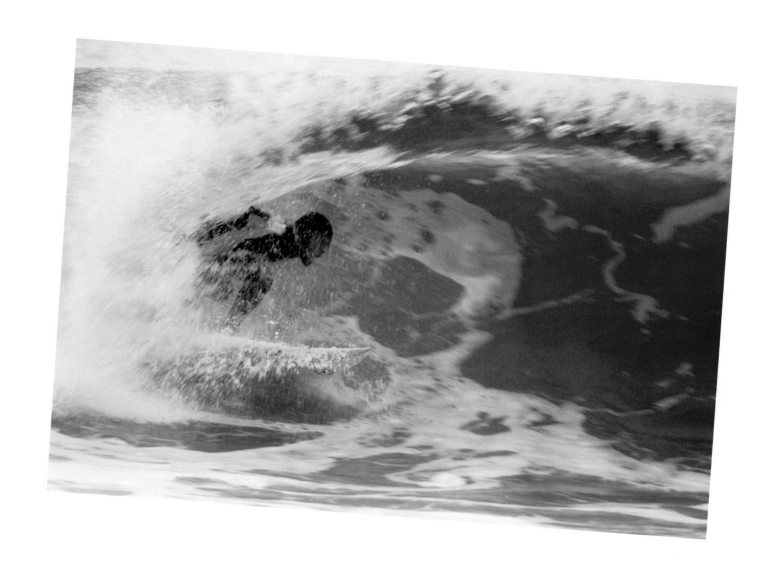

tosha Santosha

Santosha

Santosha

If the sport of surfing has a goal, it's to find the Perfect Wave. The holy grail of all waveriders is to find cartoon-perfect waves peeling empty and hollow along a point, or pitching over a reef to form endless rollercoaster rides. Every surfer dreams of somehow stumbling over a forgotten beach where the surf is always flawless, the breeze is always offshore and the water is always warm and the crowds are nowhere to be seen. Sometimes you get a glimpse of this utopia when conditions at your local beach come together, but it's a fleeting hint of the dream. All surfers believe that somewhere surely this mystical beach exists, and all they have to do is find it. Some are certain that somehow one day they will wander there, and in 1974 writer and surfer Larry Yates described where it was, on an island called Santosha. He described it as 'a state of mind, a state of being and a land of forgotten dreams.' A place that only exists in your head.

Travel Travel
Travel Travel

Surfing is one of the few methods left in this connected world by which you can still be a genuine explorer. You don't even need to travel very far. There are still plenty of little known or undiscovered waves even on this coast, scoured for years by surfers looking for the precious jewel of an unknown spot. That beach tucked away in a steeply sheltered cove may be flat today, it might be flat every day but there might be just that one day when the tide, wind and swell direction all come together in just the right combination that it fires perfect waves onto the beach. There is only way to know, and that's to be there when it happens. That might be down to luck, following a hunch, or following the clue left by a forgotten beach photograph in a charity shop book, or it might be down to endless pouring over Admiralty charts and isobars and working out where the waves might be and waiting for the moment. There are breaks that only work once a year, perhaps once every five years, but if you have the patience to search and the luck to find that magic combination of variables that unlocks the waves, you'll have a hidden secret.

Through The Rocks

Through The Rocks

Wave

Wave Types

Types Wave Types

Wave Types

Why do waves break like they do? Two beaches could be within sight of each other but have a vastly different waves. One could be a violently pitching shorebreak, hammering itself directly onto the sand while its neighbour could be a gentle, lazy swell, neatly reeling itself open. One would be covered with bodyboarders, pulling into the hollow closeouts unsurfable on a standup board, while the other would be full of longboarders, gracefully rollercoasting along the open face. Same swell, different beach, hugely different waves. Why so different? The shape of a wave is governed by the shape of the seabed. A wave crossing deep water is unaffected by the shape of the seabed, losing none of its energy as it approaches the shore. When that wave suddenly encounters shallow water, it will dump all that energy in one go, hurling itself forward and over into the shorebreak loved by bodyboarders. If, on the other hand, the seabed was gently sloping out into the ocean, the swell will be subtly feel it. It will warp and gently break in places before others, pulling itself over into that rolling wave best ridden old-skool style on a longboard.

113

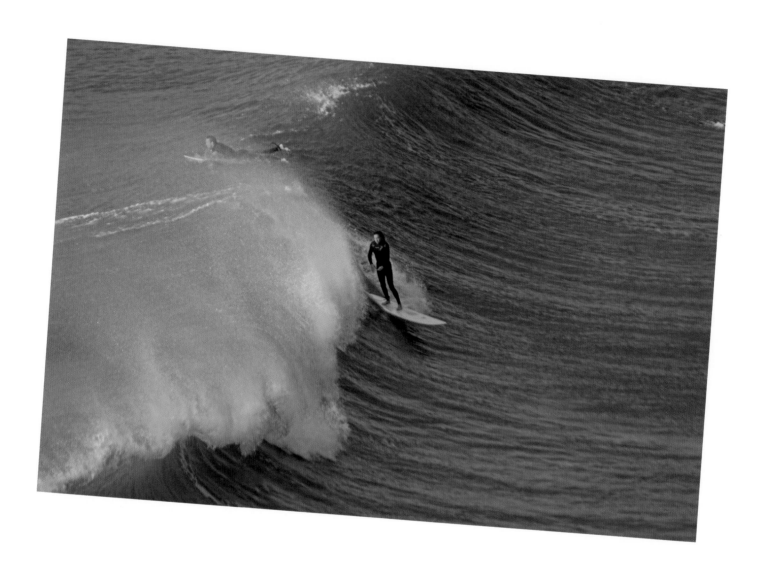

Drop Knee
Drop Knee

Barrel
Barrel

Surfers are obsessed with the weather. Get two surfers together and the conversation will within a few moments turn to critical subjects like the wind direction, the state of the tide, and whether or not that low pressure out in the mid-Atlantic is going to swing north or not. Every one a self-taught meteorological expert, we can glance at a weather chart and intepret those cryptic isobar charts into the effect it will have a the local beach. Specialist surfing websites exist that pull together data from all the world's foremost weather forecasters, combining it with live data feeds from remote wave buoys floating in mid-ocean and real-time atmospheric models. Millions of pounds worth of equipment and computing power is leeched and interrogated just to answer the one, nagging, question that is pemanently etched into the back of every surfer's mind. 'Are there any waves?'

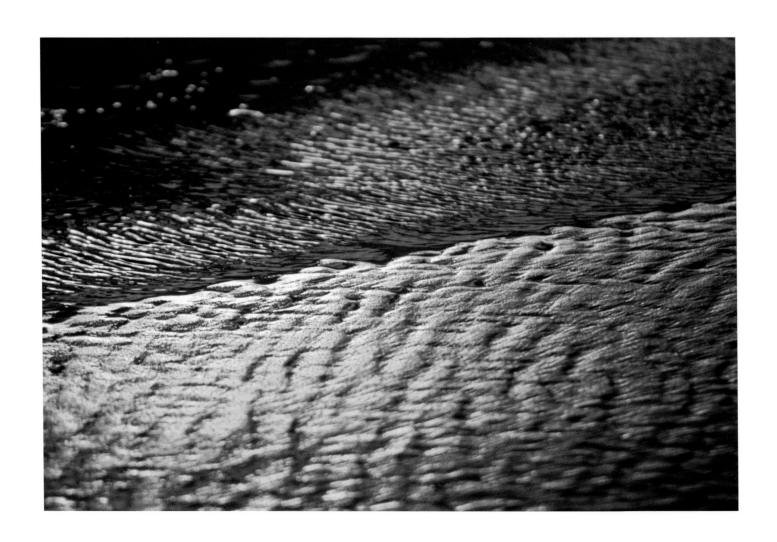